THE SAVING

OF

TUDOR HOUSE

by

A. G. K. Leonard

A G K Leonard

Cover: Tudor House c. 1902

Published for the City of Southampton Society
by
PAUL CAVE PUBLICATIONS LTD.,
74 Bedford Place, Southampton.

Published November, 1987

ISBN 0-86146-065-0

© A. G. K. Leonard 1987

Note: In the text, there
are reference notes (mainly
in brackets), a guide to which is on p. 31.

Printed by Brown & Son (Ringwood) Ltd.

TUDOR HOUSE

The plaque outside Tudor House Museum states:

"This early sixteenth century town house was built by Sir John Dawtry of Petworth and later became the residence of Sir Richard Lyster, Chief Baron of the King's Exchequer during the reign of King Henry VIII and Lord Chief Justice of the King's Bench 1546-1552. The garden gives access to the remains of a Norman merchant's house built about 1150 AD.

The house and grounds were acquired by Southampton Corporation in 1911 and opened to the public as a museum in 1912."

John Dawtry, knighted in 1515, was a burgess from 1490, MP in 1491-92 and 1495, controller of customs by 1500, victualler of the navy and organiser of town defences. He had his house (which John Leland about 1540 described as "very fair") built some years before his death in 1518, on the site of and partly incorporating several earlier houses, whose cellars remain.

Dawtry's widow Isabel married Sir Richard Lyster, whose knighthood in 1529 accompanied his appointment as Chief Baron, continuing his advancement in the service of Henry VIII that brought him a dozen Hampshire estates in the 1530s. As early as 1524 he was easily the richest man in Southampton, with at least eight servants and assessable goods worth £250. Lyster doubtless divided his time between London and his handsome house in Southampton, to which he retired in 1552 after a profitable career as "a sound but undistinguished lawyer" (DNB). He died in 1554 and was buried at St. Michael's church, opposite his home. Thirteen years later his widow (Lyster's third wife, Elizabeth Stoke) erected the canopied altar tomb and effigy of him still to be seen in St. Michael's — albeit re-sited and now lacking two sides of its original canopy.

By his will Sir Richard Lyster, who came from an old Yorkshire family, divided his properties north and south of the Trent, between his two grandsons. His Southampton house was among those bequeathed to another Richard Lyster, eldest son of his own deceased son Sir Michael Lyster. Its subsequent ownership and sub-dividing tenancies must remain shadowy, as what later became esteemed as Tudor House gradually declined in status — while local commemoration of its former owner petered out around 1700 when Lord's Lane took its present title of Blue Anchor Lane from the inn of that name. The Tudor House property nevertheless seems to have remained intact, including the grounds stretching back to the Norman House (popularly called "King John's Palace") and the arcaded town wall, into which its seaward frontage had been incorporated in the fourteenth century.

The property changed hands in 1733 for £780: thirty years later George Rogers bought it for £800. In 1795 Bryant Barrett of Stockwell, who inherited it from Rogers, sold it for £1,020 to "Peter Bernard the elder of Southampton, surgeon," from whom it passed to his sons Thomas and Peter Bernard. (They had considerable property interests in the eastward development of the town and in 1807 contributed £350 to the corporation for making a street through Pitt's Lane and building a bridge over the former town ditch and disused canal, leading to Bernard Street, which perpetuates their name.)

Ownership remained within the Bernard family until 1860, when the property was acquired by William Lankester (1798-1875, principal of the long-established firm of iron and brass founders and furnishing ironmongers, very active in Southampton's public affairs). On his death, it passed to his eldest son, William Goddard Lankester — who continued the family record of public service and besides heading the firm was also manager of the Floating Bridge Company.

In 1868 W. Lankester renewed a lease of the northern section of Tudor House and grounds along Blue Anchor Lane to George Henry Pope (whose family home had been there some twenty years — listed by the 1851 census), in business as a dyer and furniture cleaner in part of the house and various outbuildings behind it, with a shop at the front (then styled 10 St. Michael's Square). Old photographs held in Tudor House Museum (undated but probably taken about 1880) show the wall plastered over the timber framing, above an unprepossessing ground floor frontage adapted to provide entrances for three separate tenants.

The central section was then occupied by the bookbinder George Cawte but for ten years from 1883 this part (called Old Palace House, 9 St. Michael's Square) was the home and office of Josiah George Poole — who had previously lived there for some years in the 1850s. His original lease dated 8 December 1851 (of which a copy is preserved among family papers) had allowed him to "remove the present shop window and substitute a common sash window and iron fencing." J. G. Poole was an architect and surveyor, who served the corporation, Harbour Board and other public bodies; his works included restoration of the south side of the Bargate in 1864-65, the Ransom fountain at Asylum Green, the Masonic Hall in Albion Place and enlarging St. Joseph's church in 1850, after A. W. N. Pugin's beginning.

In his *Occasional Notes* (1938, 56-7) "Townsman" (E. A. Mitchell) gave a lively account of Christmas celebrations at Old Palace House, when Poole's large family (he had five children by his first wife and sixteen by his second, although not all survived infancy) gathered for dinner in the Banqueting Hall. Several inserted ceilings made it less lofty than as later restored, while the gallery was enclosed by a plaster wall separating it as part of another tenancy.

As public-spirited men, the Lankesters may have bought and held the Tudor House property with an eye to its preservation but rehabilitation and restoration had to await the arrival in Southampton of William Francis Gummer Spranger (1848-1917), a discreet and practical philanthropist and a man of sensitivity, with the means to implement it. Tudor House was his most public benefaction to his adopted town. Paying tribute to him after his death in 1917, his fellow magistrate Dr. (later Sir) Russell Bencraft said "Tudor House would be a lasting memorial to him, as it was due to his generosity and foresight that it was secured for the town" (H Adv 16 June 1917).

Public memory is notoriously short and Spranger's distinctive contribution is now overlooked in recent accounts of Tudor House Museum. The current *Southampton City*

CLEANING & DYEING

IN ALL ITS BRANCHES,

AT THE OLD ESTABLISHED SHOP,

No. 10, ST. MICHAEL'S SQUARE, SOUTHAMPTON.

Grateful for the encouragement and support he has received from the Nobility, Gentry, and Public in general, during a period of 28 years, hopes by perseverance and strict attention to the execution of work (however extensive) entrusted to him, still to merit a continuance of that support with which he has been favoured for so many years past.

Ladies' Dresses of every description Cleaned or Dyed.

BRITISH & FOREIGN SHAWLS, SCARFS, &c., CLEANED BY A PROCESS THAT WILL ENSURE THE COLOURS BEING PRESERVED.

Chintz & Printed Furniture cleaned & highly glossed,
SOFA, COUCH, & CHAIR COVERS DONE WITHOUT TAKING TO PIECES.

Moreen and Damask Furniture, Fringes, &c., Cleaned, Dyed, and Finished in a Superior manner.

ALL KINDS OF TABLE COVERS CLEANED, DYED, & PRESSED.

Blankets, Counterpanes, Carpets, Druggets, & Hearth Rugs properly cleaned.

GENTLEMEN'S WEARING APPAREL & SERVANTS' LIVERIES OF EVERY DESCRIPTION CLEANED IN A SUPERIOR STYLE.

The Black Extracted from Silk, Satin, Merino, Cloth, &c., and the Material Dyed to a variety of Patterns.

All sorts of Gloves Cleaned without any offensive smell.

EVERY DESCRIPTION OF STEAM-SHIP & YACHT BEDDING, COUCHES, MATTRESSES, &C., CLEANED AND RE-MADE.

Articles for Mourning Dyed on the Shortest Notice.

Orders by Carrier punctually attended to.

G. Pope's advertisement in Southampton directories of the 1850s.

Official Handbook makes no mention of it, while the *Visitors Guide* refers vaguely to the house as "elegantly restored by the Victorians." The Museums Curator writes of "extensive renovations at the time of its conversion into a museum in 1912" (Rance 1980, 45) and this mis-dating is followed in e.g. the booklet produced by the Southampton Tourist Guide Association and in the article on Sir Richard Lyster (FSMG Newsletter 1982). These and other references giving the erroneous impression that restoration was carried out by the Corporation after its acquisition of the property in 1911 — whereas it was actually undertaken for Spranger a decade earlier — are the more curious because successive editions of the Council's own guidebook to Tudor House Museum from 1914 onwards specifically stated:

"Tudor House and Norman House were purchased by Southampton CBC in 1911 at the instigation and during the Mayoralty of Col. Edward Bance, who was also chairman of the Estates Committee of the Corporation. That these profoundly interesting buildings have been preserved for future generations is also largely due to the admirable public spirit of W. F. G. Spranger Esq., J.P. of Springhill Court, Southampton, who bought the properties . . ., spent a large sum in restoring them and ultimately sold them to the Town at a price very much below his actual outlay on them."

The 17th edition (1957) of the Tudor House guidebook (rewritten by the then Museums Curator P.S. Peberdy) seems to have been the last to acknowledge that "this early sixteenth century house was rescued from the dangerous state of neglect into which it had fallen, by the enlightened attitude of the late W. F. G. Spranger Esq."

He bought the whole freehold property of Tudor House and Norman House from W. G. Lankester for £1,450, by conveyance dated 29 December 1886 — not long after he had settled in Southampton (SRO; conveyances and leases, Tudor House).

Opposite:

Tudor House, from a photograph taken about 1880 (courtesy Tudor House Museum).

*W. F. G. Spranger, from a painting at Richard Taunton College
(photograph from H. Spooner: A History of Taunton's School, 1968).*

W. F. G. Spranger

Following his death on 8 June 1917, the three Southampton weekly papers of 16 June devoted several columns to obituaries and accounts of Spranger's funeral at the old cemetery off Hill Lane, where he was buried beside his wife (who died in 1906) and his father in law. These gave details of his thirty years of public service to Southampton and referred to his many acts of private philanthropy but recorded little of his background beyond noting that he was born on 7 April 1848, had been educated at Oxford and lived for many years at Hursley, where he was said to have been influenced by John Keble.

Keble died in 1866 and his influence on Spranger was mainly transmitted by his supporter, Rev. Robert Jefferies Spranger (1811-88); William Francis Gummer married his daughter Mary and added her father's name to his own.

Son of Rev. Robert Spranger, who held a Lincolnshire living for thirty years until his death in 1850, R. J. Spranger was ordained in 1837 after taking his degrees through Exeter College, Oxford, where he remained as fellow and tutor in Hebrew until giving up his position in 1845 (Boase 1965, VI, 602; Crockford 1882). Evidently possessed of considerable private means, he thereafter held no office but devoted himself voluntarily to assisting Keble in providing daily services at Hursley.

Directories show him living there, at Southend House, from about 1850 until 1880; his name was sometimes printed as Sprainger, which confirms its pronunciation. In the 1860s R. J. Spranger published several volumes of theological studies, lectures and sermons. He was associated with two Southampton churches, helping with services at St. Lawrence and St. Michael's. The vicar of St. Michael's, Francis Maundy Gregory, conducted his funeral with due ritual and ceremonial; the wrought iron screens placed in the central arch and north aisle of this church in 1890 were given by the congregation as a memorial to R. J. Spranger and his wife (Cotton 1970, 25). Their son in law maintained the connection with St. Michael's, as churchwarden and benefactor.

W. F. G. Spranger and his family of a son and two daughters presumably shared the house at Hursley, for they were not listed separately there. About 1880 R. J. Spranger moved to Brighton for the sake of his health; they may have accompanied him for a while but before 1887 they settled at Southampton, taking Windsor House, 2 Cumberland Place. R. J. Spranger was staying with them there when he died on 29 August 1888, aged 76. The *Hampshire Independent* of 8 September noted him as "a great benefactor of the poor, without regard to denomination, active in many works of benevolence and piety."

His son in law must have received a considerable inheritance, for he was able to buy Springhill Court and have it rebuilt and enlarged as a Victorian mansion, with a splendidly ornate brickwork frontage — designed by Alfred Gutteridge and built by Bull and Son, the Southampton firm whose major projects had earlier included the Law Courts in the Strand and the Parliament buildings at Cape Town as well as many sizeable local contracts.

Springhill Court in Hill Lane was originally a late 18th century country house which for fifty years accommodated an "Establishment for Young Gentlemen" ("each pupil has a single bed") run by Methodist ministers but in 1883 reverted to a private residence. Contrasting pictures of it about 1850 and 1900 were reproduced with J. Vale's article in Proc HFC 39, 182-3. The latter was taken from Pike (1905, 33), in which it was described as "a handsome modern mansion surrounded by beautifully laid out grounds." It doubtless pleased Spranger's historical sensibilities that these contained the ancient Conduit Head over the Colwell Spring, the original source of Southampton water supply by the Franciscan Friars Minor about 1290. After Spranger's death in 1917 Springhill changed hands and remained a private residence until acquired in 1923 by the Sisters of Nazareth for their boys orphanage. While this was evacuated in 1940 the buildings were destroyed by enemy action — replaced in the 1950s by the present Nazareth House. Part of the grounds ("Spranger's Field") became the site of Springhill RC school, opened in 1929.

The Sprangers moved into their reconstructed mansion in 1893. A writer in the *Southampton Times* (16 June 1917) described it as "the biggest house in town" but remarked on its "homeliness" and the modest and unassuming personality of its owner, who was genial and jocular, yet dignified, and unostentatious in his wealth — apart from wearing a huge diamond ring, which may have had sentimental family significance. The ST obituary (preferred for quotation because this radical Liberal journal was more likely than others to have given an objective appraisal of a man with Conservative connections) said that "no townsman of late years has been better known and none has been in higher repute for amiable qualities and good works."

For the last thirty years of his life Spranger devoted his energies and means to serving Southampton, involving himself with many local societies and institutions, particularly in the sphere of education.

He was first elected to the School Board in 1892, soon becoming its vice-chairman and in 1898 succeeding Canon Scannell as chairman; he held this position until the Board was superseded in 1902 by the Education Committee of the borough council — of which he was the first vice-chairman. He was elected a councillor in the Conservative interest for Banister ward in 1895, returned unopposed in 1898 and 1901 but in 1902 he resigned. Although he remained president of the ward Conservative Association, Spranger probably had little liking for divisive local politics, preferring more direct forms of public service. He was a conscientious JP from 1899 right up to his death in 1917.

Spranger was closely associated with Hartley College, as a governor and benefactor who helped promote its advancement as a University College (Temple Patterson 1962, 106, 125). He was also chairman of the committee for the (then independent) School of Art. His interest in local history brought him into the Hampshire Field Club, which he served as president in 1904-5, and he was the first chairman of the Southampton Record Society.

In 1898 he was appointed a governor of the "Endowed Schools" — Taunton's and King Edward VI — and in 1905 became chairman of the governing body, holding the office for the rest of his life. He was especially involved with Taunton's School (Spooner 1968, 180 etc), where one of the "houses" was named after him in 1908; his portrait is still displayed in present-day Richard Taunton College. In 1910 he presented the Spranger Cup for athletics and swimming, while from 1907 he gave practical encouragement to school sports by making available part of the grounds of Springhill Court to serve as the school's first "home ground". The owner of "Spranger's Field" was generous in his hospitality to Tauntonians — his strawberry and cream teas for the cricketers are still recalled. Spranger also played a key role in securing the site for the school's much-needed new buildings; he stepped in and bought five acres of the "Highfield Uplands" estate in 1913, transferring it two years later to the corporation.

Spranger enjoyed all his activities bringing him into contact with children and young people. To the younger ones he handed out sweets (sometimes in the middle of lessons!); older children received new sixpences, while he talked to them about their future prospects and afterwards sought out and gave them the books they needed. Later they might benefit from his gifts or loans to help continue their studies or enter a worthwhile career. Spranger liked to do good privately but it was recognised — as the *Hampshire Advertiser* wrote (16 June 1917) — that "many holding responsible posts all over the world owe their progress chiefly to Mr. Spranger who gave them their chance. He spent the biggest part of his life looking out for promising boys and then putting them in the way of carving a career for themselves by creating educational avenues for them."

In true story-book style, Spranger's last death-bed message was to the boys of the Endowed Schools — "lead good lives and play straight." For his funeral at St. Michael's, the church troop of boy scouts formed a guard of honour and at the cemetery the path to his grave was lined by boys of Taunton's and King Edward VI Schools.

Restoration

The plan accompanying the 1886 conveyance of the Tudor House and Norman House property from W. G. Lankester to W. F. G. Spranger showed the latter leased to Mr. Beavis, for use as a coal yard, with a stable at the corner within Blue Anchor Lane and the medieval town wall — three arches, four buttresses and a gateway previously leased by the corporation for 19s. a year to Lankester and renewed to Spranger for 40 years from 25 March 1890.

William Beavis, tenant of the shell of the Norman House, was a partner and later principal in the firm of Haddon and Beavis, shipping agents and coal merchants of 83 High Street. Beavis, who died in 1924 aged 65 (ST 5 July 1924) was a town councillor from 1900 and alderman from 1911, an enthusiastic swimmer and chairman of the Baths committee for 21 years. He is remembered for having given the corporation £10,000 in celebration of the Armistice in 1918 (ahead of his intended bequest) as a trust fund to provide annual treats for elementary school children (SRO TC Misc 17): Beavis Treat money now subsidises educational journeys by middle school pupils.

Spranger must soon have gained control of the Norman House and put its restoration in hand, for he was able to show the renovated building to "a very large number of members of the Hampshire Field Club" attending "an afternoon in Old Southampton" on 23 October 1890 and to entertain them to tea "in the upstair room of this interesting old building . . . the central attraction of the day's programme . . . which has just undergone a process of judicious restoration . . . to preserve it as one of the sights of the town" (H Adv, 25 October 1890).

The HFC editor (Proc 2, 367) afterwards wrote an account of the Norman House, concluding:
"It is mainly owing to the public spirit of Mr. W. F. G. Spranger, who acquired the

property, and to the late Mr. T. K. Dymond, both members of the H.F.C., that this almost unique specimen of early domestic architecture has been preserved. Mr. Dymond, an enthusiastic antiquary, gave unremitting attention to the restoration, in which he was assisted by Mr. E. Cooper Poole, architect.

The premises, which had been occupied as a coal store and stable, were cleaned; the round-headed doorway in Blue Anchor Lane was opened; windows, which had long been blocked, once more admitted the light, and this ancient building has been rendered accessible to inspection. It is now placed under the care of an intelligent custodian, who will gladly show it to any who may be interested in objects of antiquity.''

On site in 1890, H.F.C. members had felt "it is a matter of congratulation when such an interesting heirloom of the past comes into the hands of an enlightened owner, who will do his best to preserve it for posterity.''

Spranger had the walls covered with canvas, on which were hung copies of parts of the Bayeux tapestry, and put a miscellany of relics on show in the upper chamber. Herbert Oakley's drawing (Proc 2, 365) suggests that these included the sixteenth century "treasure chest" which Spranger later presented to Tudor House Museum, where it now serves to collect visitors' contributions. Another museum exhibit, the sedan chair formerly belonging to the Marett family of old Westgate House, was noted in 1898 by Rev. G. W. Minns (Proc 4, 87) as "still to be seen, with other curiosities which form the furniture of the upper chamber of the Norman House.'' Spranger had evidently made it a sort of private museum.

With unsightly whitewash cleaned off them, the roof beams aroused keen interest among H.F.C. members on their visit in 1890, when they speculated on the age of the timbers. Some even thought them original, although this seems unlikely. In his *Walk through Southampton* (1801) Sir Henry Englefield wrote of the Norman House in terms suggesting it then had no floor dividing it into two storeys but there is no indication that floor or roof were part of Spranger's restoration. Either or both may have been of comparatively recent date (perhaps re-using timber from another old building), relating to use of the building as a tenement and store. Large-scale maps of 1870 onwards are inconclusive in establishing whether all or only part of the Norman House was roofed over; some shaded areas may represent sheds and stables.

Both roof and floor seem to have been removed some time before 1911-12 — perhaps because they had become unsafe. The only reference so far traced is in an article by E. A. Mitchell (Townsman 1938, 11): "Up to recent times this building was used as a dwelling house. There are among older generations of Sotonians those who remember well when it contained its upper room, in which certain relics were kept and which was sheltered by a timber roof. That was before it was taken over by the Corporation, together with Tudor House. But prior to this latter event, the roof and floor had vanished and the place had been reduced to a roofless shell, exposed to wind and rain.'' There is now a corporation proposal to give it a modern lightweight, perhaps transparent, roof, which would provide an enclosed space admirably suited for dramatic representations exemplifying the long history of the structure Spranger was responsible for preserving nearly a century ago.

The dating of the restoration of Tudor House is less certain; contemporary references are fragmentary but it must have been a protracted (and costly) process, probably extending over the years 1898-1902. Spranger had to wait for leases to expire or be

Edward Cooper Poole, from a portrait painted in 1921 by his friend, V. C. Batalha Reis ARIBA, Portuguese vice-consul at Southampton for twenty years between the wars. It was donated to Tudor House in 1986 by his daughter-in-law, Mrs. M. Cooper-Poole. (Photograph by Tom Holder).

terminated before internal rehabilitation and exterior reconstruction could be put in hand. When he bought the property in 1886, the St. Michael's Street frontage of what was "formerly one capital messuage, now two dwelling houses" was shown on the conveyance plan (SRO) as divided between four tenants — John James Carter (who had replaced Pope the dyer) along Blue Anchor Lane; Josiah George Poole, occupying the central part styled Old Palace House; and two others named Kitto and Pim (the latter holding the cottage in Bugle Street adjoining the south side of the main Tudor building which had been part of the property since George Rogers brought it in 1764).

These tenants left after a few years. Pope and Co. were last listed at 10 St. Michael's Square in 1888, Poole and Son in 1891. J. G. Poole, then in failing health, spent his last years in a house at Gordon Avenue, dying in 1897. About this time his son, Edward Cooper Poole, took a house in Hill Lane but may have continued at Old Palace House for a while after his father left, although he had transferred his office to Portland Street by 1892.

E. C. Poole AMICE FRIBA took over his father's work for the Harbour Board from 1887 and served as its engineer and architect (initially part-time, full-time from 1916) for 48 years, until his death in 1935 — a few weeks before he would have retired at 70 (H Adv 17 August 1935, Kimber 1948, 173-6).

He designed the Board's new offices, opened by Admiral Earl Jellicoe on 8 September 1925, and the entrance to the Royal Pier, reconstructed in 1926-27 (replacing the more mundane buildings for which he had been responsible in 1890-92). One would like to think that the present frontage of Tudor House came from the same drawing board as this whimsically attractive composition.

Tudor House Museum has today no record of the architect responsible for its present appearance. The papers and memories of the Cooper-Poole family, several of whom long cherished their connection with Old Palace House (John Cooper-Poole, a grandson of Edward Cooper Poole, drew neat sketches of the building for the Tudor House Museum guidebook, 1957 edition) cannot now provide confirmation, so there is only circumstantial evidence to link E. Cooper Poole with the restoration of Tudor House. Even if only on an informal basis, it seems inherently likely that he was Spranger's architect, for his family home was part of the property when Spranger bought it and for some years after; he was clearly Spranger's architect for restoring the Norman House in 1890; and he was a member of the H.F.C., to which in 1888 he contributed a drawing of "The Bridewell Gate and South Castle" (Proc 1, facing 61).

However the credit for the restoration of Tudor House be apportioned between client and architect, it was sensitively accomplished, avoiding romantic excesses and devoting much care to detail and verisimilitude, to get as near to the original as could be conceived, keeping conjectural additions and replacements to the minimum and seeking to recreate and highlight the integrity of the Tudor structure, which had been obscured by later additions and alterations. The restoration provided a new ground floor frontage in seemingly authentic Tudor style; above it, plaster was removed to reveal timbers and brickwork. Inside, there must have been many plaster and partition additions to remove. Some old features were revealed, others renewed.

"The show facade to Bugle Street is in general appearance as Dawtrey built it, but with a great deal of detailed restoration, much of it faithfully copying original features (as comparison with pre-restoration photographs proves), but some of it is straightforward neo-Tudor, where the original features had been obliterated'' write Pevsner and Lloyd (1967, 530) — whose expert overall verdict is ''thoroughly but, on the whole, commendably restored.''

The only account of the work by Spranger himself seems to be the interview he gave in 1911 (ST 21 Jan 1911). He was reported as saying that he had acquired the property with the object of preserving it and that some years later ''the Tudor House had got into such a ruinous state that extensive repairs were imperatively necessary. A leading firm of local builders were commissioned to do these repairs, which gradually developed into complete restoration.'' If Spranger then mentioned the names of his builder and architect, they were not recorded.

Spranger explained that ''the original building had undergone changes in the course of the centuries which he had no knowledge of when the builders' men were set to work. Externally, herring-bone brickwork had been covered over with stucco and characteristic timbering of the Tudor period was hidden in many parts. Inside, some very remarkable discoveries were made. Lath and plaster ceilings had been fixed below the original ceilings of panelled oak, great chestnut beams had been similarly hidden, windows blocked up, fire-places altered and many of the principal beauties, as now visible, defaced and despoiled.''

''Every new find'', said Mr. Spranger, ''was a great temptation to go on and I spent so much money having things put as right as possible again that I was compelled to pull myself up.'' When he ''had done almost everything that was to be done in the way of putting the place into a thoroughly good state'' he offered it to the Corporation in 1905.

Spranger must have initiated work at Tudor House before 1900. Around 1898 the northern part was briefly occupied by J. J. Myers, a printer's engraver, while the central section was shown in directories of 1898-1900 as accommodating a coffee house run by David Harris — perhaps catering for visitors.

At the borough council meeting in November 1898, Spranger had denounced fellow members whose ''utilitarian'' views favoured granting building leases across the demolished section of the town wall after removal of West Gate House — ''they were regarded by outsiders as perfect Goths and Vandals'' — and in a rare personal reference said ''he had put himself to considerable expense in the preservation of the Norman House and if a private individual could make sacrifices in that way the council ought to be prepared to do a little'' (ST 19 Nov 1898). Spranger does not then seem to have made any similar public mention of his role in repairing and restoring Tudor House — which evidently cost him four or five times what he originally paid for the property.

Contemporary references to the progress of this work are fragmentary. In the 1900 edition of *Mate's Illustrated Guide to Southampton* Rev. G. N. Godwin described Tudor House as ''a handsome timber-framed building (which) has lately been restored in perfect good taste'' (Godwin, 1900, unpaged). This historian would have known Spranger and what he was doing at Tudor House, so his use of the past tense may have anticipated completion of the work there. The *Southampton Annual* for 1901 carried forward the first part of a paragraph from its 1899 and 1900 editions — ''Once upon a time the old Tudor House was famous enough. Alas, the glory of it is now gone'' — but amended the next sentence to say ''All the neighbourhood was squalid and slummy but the

Picture postcard of Tudor House, F. G. O. Stuart; photograph taken 1903 or earlier.

Corporation and the owner have restored to Tudor House something of its ancient prestige and aided in its preservation.'' The Corporation contribution involved slum clearance, the erection of the first "council houses" and a public lodging house — St. Michael's House, officially opened by the mayor on 27 October 1899, demolished in 1972.

The H.F.C. Annual Report for 1901 (Proc 4, 2) noted a meeting at Southampton on 17 October 1901: "A visit to the Tudor House in St. Michael's Square drew forth the praise and admiration of all present. The public spirit of the present owner, Mr. W. F. G. Spranger, a member of our Society, in effecting such an excellent restoration was highly commended.''

The captions to photographs of Tudor House in the *Southampton Annual* of 1900 (48) describe it as "restored" but they show the frontage only as tidied up from its earlier nondescript state, not yet reconstructed, with timbers supporting the porch. The 1901 edition showed this porch made good but the old inserted central doorway still remains. These photographs may, of course, have been taken some time before publication.

When the exterior of Tudor House was restored to its present appearance it quickly became an attractive subject for picture postcard publishers. Locally pre-eminent among them was F. G. O. Stuart (a Scot settled in Southampton), who began issuing cards in the latter part of 1901, drawing on his large stock of prints previously supplied to various guidebook and periodical publishers. A photograph of Tudor House, fully reconstructed externally as it has appeared for over eighty years, was used for Stuart cards numbered 613 and 650, the first British-printed in black and white, the second coloured and produced in Germany. The earliest postmarks so far noted on examples of these cards are respectively 10 June 1903 and 1 March 1904: the photograph(s) must have been taken earlier in 1903, perhaps in 1902, thus providing useful pointers to the date of completion of the external restoration of Tudor House.

16

Edward Bance

At the borough council meeting in November 1898 Spranger had suggested (ST 19 Nov 1898) that "the old guard house by the West Gate might come in very well for the purposes of a small museum of objects of historical interest." (Preservation of this fifteenth century building, restored in 1973-75 as "Tudor Merchants Hall", was largely due to H.F.C. members supporting the undertaking made in 1899 by Rev. G. W. Minns to raise £100 to supplement the £50 which was all the corporation would then agree to spend on repairs).

While Spranger may not have originally envisaged Tudor House as a museum, opinion that it should be so used gathered strength in 1904, centred on the successful "Grand Loan Exhibition of Relics of Old Southampton, illustrating the ancient life and history of the borough" held at Hartley University College from 12 to 17 September that year.

Its "originator and leading spirit" was Professor F. J. C. Hearnshaw, who powerfully promoted the study of local history: his initiative and energy were mainly responsible for the formation of the Southampton Record Society in 1905 — "his most important legacy to Southampton" (Temple Patterson, 1962, 113). Spranger was its first chairman. As president of the H.F.C. he was also vice-chairman of the committee responsible for organising the 1904 "Relics" exhibition; the chairman was Alderman Edward Gayton, then chairman of the Hartley Council.

The exhibition, crammed into rooms in the College building, brought together a mass of items from the Hartley collection, corporation archives and some eighty private owners: Spranger's contribution was the treasure chest previously mentioned. Open for six full days, the exhibition drew 7,500 visitors, paying 6d or 1s. Organised classes of schoolchildren were admitted for 2d. Many people attended the free lectures given during the week by Hearnshaw, Shore and others and paid 3d to join the parties conducted twice daily around Tudor House, King John's Palace and the Undercroft by Charles Cooksey and William Dale.

The financial success of the exhibition enabled the organisers to publish in cheap popular form a substantial book (Hearnshaw 1904) containing an annotated catalogue of the exhibits, the texts of nine lectures and a report of the speeches made at the opening meeting, when Lord Montagu of Beaulieu and others had highlighted Southampton's need of a permanent museum.

There was general agreement with Alderman Gayton — "it does seem a great pity that these exhibits . . . should be lost to the town, whose history they chronicle . . . True, they are only loaned but if a permanent museum were established would there not be many possessors of ancient relics who would be willing to help furnish a museum which would be a credit to the town?" Several commendatory references were made to Spranger's restoration of Tudor House and Rev. G. W. Minns evidently expressed a growing consensus when "He trusted that at no distant date they might have the treasures of the Hartley museum deposited in some local museum worthy of the collection . . . and a haven for the deposit of articles which collectors would readily give if there were a prospect of the objects being preserved with proper care. He suggested that Tudor House (so well restored by Mr. Spranger, to whom all lovers of antiquity in Southampton owed a debt of gratitude) . . . at present unused, would make an excellent museum."

In his introduction to the hastily compiled catalogue of the exhibition Hearnshaw wrote with apologetic modesty "It is too much to expect, perhaps, that it should give any help towards the formation of a Southampton Museum, similar to that which exists in Winchester, in Salisbury and indeed in most towns which have anything of a history behind them. But there is no doubt that the formation of such a museum is an ideal which all who love Southampton and feel an interest in its noble annals should keep steadily before them. One may venture to dream as one stands amid the relics of the past — now for the first time gathered together and soon to be dispersed — of such a collection permanently enshrined in some such magnificent abode as the Tudor House."

These sentiments received civic support from the Mayor, Alderman Edward Bance DL, JP, who formally reported to the Estates Committee of the Borough Council on 7 February 1905 that "he had been approached in reference to the desirability of providing a museum for the town" (SBCM 1905, 306).

Then serving the second of his three terms as mayor, Bance (1842-1925: S Ref 17 July 1880, ST and H Adv 11 July 1925) was for forty years a prominent figure in the public life of the town. Southampton-born, of Huguenot descent, he received a commercial education and began his many-sided career as a "computor" — a civilian member of the computing and surveying staff of the Ordnance Survey, undertaking complicated calculations and arduous field work. He left the OS at 24, to establish his own extensive business as surveyor, valuer, estate agent and auctioneer; from 1885 he was principal of the firm of Bance, Hunt and Co., with imposing offices in Above Bar.

As a young man, his efficiency as secretary of the Athenaeum and other local societies gained wider recognition of his abilities, which were further applied in public service from 1874, when he was first elected a councillor for St. Mary's ward. Becoming an alderman in 1889, he continued prominent in council affairs until his retirement in 1913, thrice serving as mayor — in 1891-2, 1904-5 and 1910-11.

Plaques on the parapet at each end of Central Bridge, erected in 1882, note his role as chairman of the corporation committee which eventually persuaded the LSWR to build what was popularly known as "Bance's Bridge" to supersede the level crossing which had long impeded Southampton traffic. Bance played an important part in many other matters central to the development of the town and port and was involved with several local companies as chairman or director. He was an active Liberal, for 26 years chairman of the company publishing the Radical weekly *Southampton Times,* but declined an invitation to stand for Parliament in 1895.

His appointment as a Deputy Lieutenant of the County recognised his service in the 1st Hants Volunteer Artillery, of which he was a member for 33 years, joining as a gunner in 1863, commissioned in 1872 and given command the following year. Colonel Bance built up the corps from 60 to 800 trained men (notwithstanding — or perhaps on account of — his "habitual propriety of speech" and insistence on "Sunday School language" at Volunteer camps) and was the first to receive the Volunteer Decoration. He was the prime mover in building the drill hall in St. Mary Street, recently given a new lease of usefulness as a sports hall.

Southampton Art Gallery has an oil painting of Bance (by H. C. Oakley), presented to him in 1906, after his second mayoralty, as "a memento of the high appreciation entertained by his fellow townsmen of his devoted and exemplary services to his native town." In the illuminated book of subscribers' signatures — widely representative of all aspects of Southampton life — that of W. F. G. Spranger heads the list.

Although differing in their politics, Bance and Spranger must in many ways have been

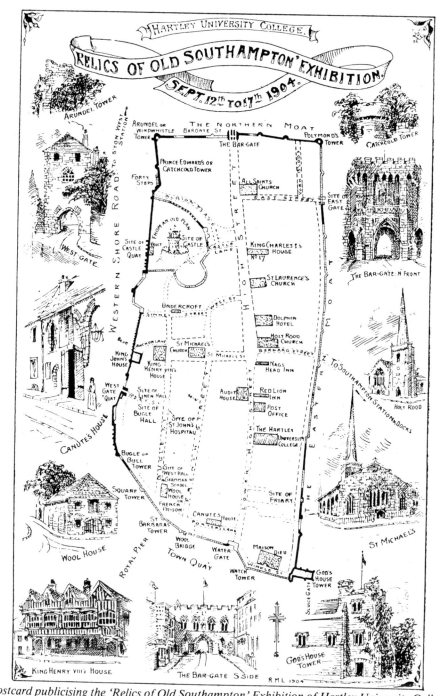

Postcard publicising the 'Relics of Old Southampton' Exhibition of Hartley University College, 12-17 September 1904, drawn by R. M. Lucas.

19

kindred spirits. Certainly they shared a common concern about Tudor House. When Alderman Bance was made a Freeman of the Borough in 1912, Tudor House was prominently depicted on the ornate silver casket holding his presentation scroll — perhaps at his own suggestion, perhaps proposed by others who wished to note his success in eventually securing its acquisition by the Corporation. This handsome casket, afterwards donated by his son to its successor, is now displayed in the Mayor's Parlour at the Civic Centre.

Bance's association with the "Relics of Old Southampton" exhibition must have deepened his interest in the town's history and antiquities, already expressed through his efforts over the years as chairman of the council's Estates Committee to recover parts of the old walls and towers as leases fell in on those previously leased by the Corporation to private tenants. Much impressed by what he had seen at York, "he trusted that eventually the whole of the remains would return to the possession of the town, so that some day they might be enabled to take a walk round the old walls." He also hoped that "other valuable remains would be opened up to public view" (speech of thanks to Hearnshaw and exhibition organisers, 12 September 1904; Hearnshaw 1904, 18).

The suggestion of a town museum, as mooted by Bance, was initially referred to a sub-committee of the Estates Committee. On its report, the committee decided on 7 March 1905 (SBCM 1905, 414) to ask the Public Libraries Committee to consider establishing a museum at the Central Public Library. (This 1893 building, on the site of the former New Place House at the foot of Bedford Place/London Road, was destroyed by bombing in 1940).

Council minutes (1905, 798, 954) indicate that discussions, in which the Mayor took part, were held between representatives of the two committees and that in July the Public Libraries Committee "approved of the suggested establishment of a public museum at the Central Library" but they do not record the process by which this proposal was soon set aside in favour of the acquisition of Tudor House for museum purposes. Lack of accommodation at the Library was the likeliest explanation; perhaps Bance wanted to get this recognised before guiding the Estates Committee on 1 August 1905 (SBCM 1905, 954) to adopt a resolution instructing the Town Clerk to ask Mr. Spranger "whether he would be prepared to let or sell Tudor House, King John's Palace and the whole of the premises therewith for the purpose of a public museum and if so, upon what terms."

Bance must have been in touch with Spranger and had some idea of his likely response to such an approach. This was soon given, in a letter of 11 August from his solicitors, Messrs. Sharp, Harrison, Turner and Cooper (printed in SBCM 1905, 956-7) stating that "he will be pleased to treat with the Corporation for the sale or lease of this property and in view of the object for which it is proposed to be used, he is prepared to make a substantial reduction in his terms."

"The property covers a considerable area of ground and consists of:-
1. Tudor House and garden, with the small house adjoining and forming part of the Frontage to Bugle Street, let to Mr. Cooper at £19 per annum.
2. King John's Palace and a stable and yard adjoining, let to Mr. Tilling at £14 per annum."

(G. J. Tilling was a coal merchant and ship supplier, member of the borough council, Mayor in 1899-1900).

"Mr. Spranger is willing either to sell the first-named property alone, or to sell both the afore-mentioned properties. If the former is only desired, he fixes the purchase price at £3,200. For the two properties his price is £4,200."

Edward Bance, from a photgraph taken in 1880, when he was 38
(from Southern Reformer, 17 July 1880).

The letter added "We should mention that the whole property has cost Mr. Spranger about £8,000 and in view of this, he trusts that in naming the foregoing terms it will be recognised that he is making a liberal concession in favour of the Town."

The Estates Committee evidently agreed. At its meeting on 5 September it resolved comprehensively "to recommend the Council to accept the offer of Mr. Spranger and to purchase the two properties for the sum of £4,200; that the necessary application be made to the Local Government Board for sanction to borrow that amount; and that a provisional contract be entered into for the purchase of the properties" (SBCM 1905, 957).

It also resolved to recommend the Council to adopt the Museums and Gymnasiums Act, 1891. This would enable it to spend up to the product of a halfpenny rate "to provide and maintain museums for the reception of local antiquities or other objects of interest" — to be open to the public free of charge not less than three days a week: for the rest, the Council could charge admission fees and also grant use of the premises for any purpose of education or instruction.

On 8 September the Town Clerk gave formal notice (SBCM 1905, 993) that at the Council meeting on 11 October a resolution would be put to adopt the 1891 Act, to come into operation a month thereafter. In advance of that, the Council meeting of 13 September received the report of the Estates Committee. Item 17, Public Museum, proved contentious. The three Southampton weekly papers of 16 September gave full and almost identical reports of the debate ensuing.

Proposing adoption, the Mayor, as committee chairman, said Tudor House was one of the finest specimens of its age; Mr. Spranger's offer was most liberal; it was "most desirable" to obtain the property and utilize it as a public museum — and also as a supplementary reading room and public library, especially now the Hartley College facilities were no longer available to the public. Alderman Bance said the interest upon the expenditure would be £178 a year; furnishing the museum would cost about £800, so that the total interest would be some £200 a year. He recognised that maintenance would be another matter but one of the town sergeants could live over the premises and the museum could be made "practically self-supporting."

The seconder was Councillor John Haysom (partner in the firm of Garret and Haysom, monumental masons, a public-spirited man of wide interests); he stressed that the Tudor House project would be a real benefit to the town, especially for the younger generation, and would attract visitors.

Councillor Weston led the voices taking a contrary view; the town could not afford it, so the offer could not be entertained — maintenance and staffing would cost £500 a year. Alderman Dunsford thought the time was "not opportune": Alderman Edward Gayton (a High Street wine merchant), who as chairman of the Hartley Council the previous September had seemed to support establishing a permanent town museum, agreed, saying that while some American would jump at the chance of buying Tudor House, even for £8,000, the Corporation was not in a position to acquire it. Councillor Cheverton echoed the view that the town could not afford it but was sure Mr. Spranger would allow any interested citizen to inspect Tudor House. Councillor George Parker's expression "this is the time to take the property by the forelock" elicited much laughter — in which the Mayor can hardly have joined, for he was obliged to say that if the Council cared nothing about the ancient relics of the town, he had done, but he had considered it his duty to bring forward this important matter of a museum at Tudor House.

Earlier, Councillor Hamilton had congratulated him on what he had done, when seconding a motion by Labour spokesman "Tommy" Lewis that the question of acquiring Tudor House be deferred until the Council considered adopting the 1891 Act — not because he was against it but because he wanted the whole matter of museums and gymnasiums to be properly discussed.

Lewis's motion was carried on a show of hands. Then Alderman Le Feuvre, seconded by Gayton, proposed an amendment "that this Council does not fail to appreciate the generosity shown by Mr. Spranger in offering to part with Tudor House for so small a sum as that named but that in the present condition of the rates of the town they regret they are unable to take advantage of it." Le Feuvre said the museum project would cost £1,000 a year, which the town could not afford. Councillor Beavis (the coal merchant previously mentioned as Spranger's former tenant) boldly suggested "why not ask Mr. Spranger to present the property to the town free?" Alderman Walton urged that it should be a national property or it could pass into the hands of a building speculator. Finally, Councillor Blakeway denied that acquisition was a matter of "now or never": "Mr. Spranger was a gentleman who knew all about the value of antiquities" — the implication was that Tudor House and King John's Palace would be safe with him, even if the Council did nothing.

Le Feuvre's amendment not to purchase was carried 21-16. This vote must have involved some splitting within the Conservative-Ratepayers group, reflected in the editorial of the following Saturday's *Hampshire Advertiser*. This rated the matter "by far the most important business" of the Council meeting and said that it must be a matter of general regret that it came to nothing. Praising Mr. Spranger for being "exceedingly generous and liberal", it noted that the idea of a museum had been in mind for a long time and that the 1904 exhibition at the Hartley College had placed it more prominently before the public.

The *Advertiser* considered Tudor House and King John's Palace as "gems which ought to be in the possession of the town at any cost" and said "We ought not to leave even a chance of losing what it would be absolutely impossible to replace." Money spent buying them would be well invested and would bring more visitors. The Council had "shirked the responsibility" of undertaking it but "it is to be hoped that some other means will come to the rescue and secure this valuable prize to the town for ever." The Radical *Southampton Times* gave the fullest account of the Council debate under the heading "Public Museum — Economy Triumphant" but offered no comment. The *Hampshire Independent* (Liberal) opined with some acidity that "times are never opportune for anything in Southampton" and condemned the Corporation for failing to see the educational value of a museum; members were recommended to visit the museums at Reading, Salisbury and Dorchester, which might alter their opinion.

At the next meeting of the Council on 11 October the Mayor said there was a general (i.e. majority) opinion that nothing could be done about adopting the Museums and Gymnasiums Act at the present time and therefore he formally withdrew the motion of which notice had previously been given.

The *Avertiser* (14 October) now sided with the majority, still expressing regret but saying "it is a matter of cost merely and under all the circumstances it would be unjustifiable to incur unnecessary expenditure." The *Independent* of the same date repeated its jibe "the time is never opportune" and commented that "Southampton even yet requires some education as to safeguarding its ancient treasures and so disposing them that they shall be able to tell their interesting stories to the present and future generations."

Corporation

This process of education may have gone forward in some circles over the next few years but the matter of Tudor House did not come before the Council again until after Colonel Bance had begun his third mayoralty in November 1910. Meanwhile, the building was looked after by Spranger's resident caretaker, who opened it to visitors on request: it was also made available to St. Michael's church for various parish functions (information from Mr. G. M. W. Cotton).

Towards the end of 1910 Spranger sharpened the issue of its future by putting up a "For Sale" notice outside Tudor House. In an interview (ST 21 Jan 1911) he explained that "he had fully made up his mind to dispose of it to the highest bidder since there appeared to be no inclination on the part of the town to take it over at a reasonable price." When asked why he did not present it to the town, he replied "Because I have done something, can I be expected to do everything?" and added "I would prefer at any time to accept a reasonable price from the Corporation rather than a fancy price from any other buyer but I feel that I cannot hold the matter over indefinitely."

Spranger said that his words were not to be taken as "by way of coaxing the Corporation to deal with me for the property" but they must have had some effect when published in the *Southampton Times* (with which Bance was closely connected as chairman of the publishing company), particularly as its same issue "splashed" an eloquent letter from Gambier Bolton raising alarm about the future of Tudor House and King John's Palace.

Then well known as a world traveller, zoologist, animal photographer and popular writer and lecturer on natural history subjects, Bolton wrote from "Westbourne House, Millbrook Road and Royal Southampton Yacht Club" to alert "my fellow townsmen of all classes" to "the news, now an open secret, that enquiries from persons outside the town are at this moment being made with a view not only to the purchase but, sad to relate, the removal from England of these two ancient buildings."

He urged another approach to the town council — "I would suggest that we not only plead the urgency of prompt action in order to save these historic buildings from removal but also that they should be purchased as a memorial for all time to our late King" (Edward VII died 6 May 1910). Bolton wanted Tudor House used as a museum, "for which it is admirably suited and which is sorely needed", and the Palace to remain as it was, "both being free to the public for ever."

Should this approach fail, he envisaged a public appeal to purchase the buildings and vest them in trustees for the benefit of the town on similar lines, although it would then be necessary to make a charge to visitors. This proved not to be necessary for the borough council was sufficiently prompted by public opinion to take a more positive attitude than in 1905.

One cannot now be sure whether there was indeed a prospective American buyer intent on dismantling Southampton's historic treasures for re-erection on the other side of the

Atlantic but the possibility doubtless helped to concentrate the minds of members of the Council.

Still strategically placed as chairman of the Estates Committee, the Mayor, Alderman Bance, was minuted as reporting to its meeting of 7 February that Mr. Spranger "had been offered a higher price than that at which he had previously offered it to the Corporation" but that he still adhered to his original offer, as set out in his solicitors' letter of August 1905, which was resubmitted (SBCM 1911, 215). Bance suggested that "the committee should seriously consider the desirability of acquiring the property under the Museums and Gymnasiums Act, 1891."

He was doubtless persuasive and his committee now receptive, for it voted (with two abstentions, none against) in the simplest of terms "to recommend the Council to adopt the 1891 Act and enter into a provisional contract for the purchase of the two properties" (SBCM 1911, 216).

There was more debate when this recommendation came before the Council on 15 March — fully reported in the local newspapers of 18 March. Letters of support were reported from the Society of Antiquaries, Southampton Camera Club and the Chamber of Commerce and the Mayor strongly urged that the opportunity be taken to acquire "an exceptional property at an exceptional price." He was supported by Councillor Lewis — who hoped Hartley College would transfer some of its exhibits to the proposed new town museum.

Opposition to spending ratepayers' money on Tudor House was headed by Councillor Henry Bowyer RNR and Councillor S. G. Kimber (newly elected for Portswood ward the previous November to begin his 38 years of public life). Kimber said no one was more fond than he of the history of Tudor House but it would be better to leave the matter alone at the present time.

Moreover, he felt the town should have a museum in conjunction with a new town hall and spending money on Tudor House would simply be driving another nail in the coffin of the proposed town hall.

The recommendation of the Estates Committee was endorsed by a vote of 26 to 16 but the matter was not allowed to rest there. For the next meeting of the Council on 12 April, Councillor Henry Bowyer gave notice of motion to rescind this resolution.

Consideration was preceded by the Town Clerk reading letters from the London Hampshire Society (expressing hearty support of the museum project) and the local Postmen's Federation (protesting against expenditure of ratepayer's money upon it). Bowyer argued against the "enormous cost" of buying Tudor House and making use of it, which might involve another £5,000. He said Mr. Spranger had spent several thousands trying to clear away the inside and apart from the outside shell there was little left inside at all representative of the Tudor period except a few old beams. As to King John's Palace, there was no record that King John ever stayed there, nor was there anything to show that Tudor monarchs had stayed at Tudor House. Having equated historical significance with royal association, Bowyer felt they were not justified in putting the town to the expense of buying the property, which would bring no benefit to the ratepayers. His seconder,

Councillor Hirst, likewise viewed purchase as an unjustifiable waste of public money. He said few people went to Tudor House, claiming not more than thirty had visited it during the past year: it was unsuitable for a museum.

The Council evidently did not wish to rehearse further all the well-ventilated arguments for and against acquiring Tudor House and King John's Palace. Spranger and Bance had secured solid support, reflected in the defeat of Bowyer's motion by 26 to 14, almost identical with the previous month's vote (SBCM 1911, 446, ST, H Ind, H Adv 16 April 1911).

After this decisive vote, matters proceeded with some speed. Formal loan sanction from the Local Government Board for borrowing £4,200 to cover the purchase, applied for in June, was received in November (SBCM 1911, 587; 1911-12, 68) — by which time the Estates Committee has set up a sub-committee (under Bance's chairmanship, of course) "in connection with the utilization of these premises as a museum."

Free of mayoral duties after 9 November, Bance lost little time in getting the full committee, meeting on 2 January 1912, to confirm its resolution — admirably comprehensive, albeit somewhat congested in prose style — "to recommend the establishment of a Museum at Tudor House for the exhibition of objects of the Town and County of the Town of Southampton and Hampshire interest, and that the Borough Engineer be directed to submit a plan showing the different floors, for the purpose of an inspection of the building at an early date in connection with the carrying out of any necessary repairs, the allocation of the various rooms, the laying out of the grounds, and as to the care of the building generally" (SBCM 1912, 200).

Eight days later, the committee inspected Tudor House and King John's Palace and "gave directions to the Borough Engineer for the carrying out of all necessary repairs as was deemed expedient." On 12 February the sub-committee decided to ask Rogers and Son Ltd. (Red Lodge Nursery) "to submit a scheme and estimate for laying out the grounds attached to Tudor House as an old world garden"; these were accepted a fortnight later — to cost £30, exclusive of paths! Also on 26 February the Borough Engineer was authorised to "reconstruct a staircase and install hot water apparatus for heating the ground floor staircase hall and room along the front of the building on the first floor", at an estimated cost of £70.

In May, the committee invited applications for the position of resident caretaker at Tudor House, at a weekly wage of 25s., with free accommodation, heating and lighting. Seventy were received; four married couples were interviewed on 4 June, when Mr. and Mrs. A. J. Manning were appointed.

Three weeks later the committee agreed to spend nearly £50 on painting their rooms and fitting electric light in their quarters. For better security, the Borough Engineer was instructed "to raise the wall adjoining Tudor House and abutting on to Blue Anchor Lane" — estimated cost £25. In 1913 the Estates Committee accepted the Borough Engineer's advice to heat the museum area, for preservation of the exhibits; £50 was earmarked for this, with another £50 for steps from Tudor House garden down to King John's Palace and £70 for repairs to the arches on its south side. (SBCM 1912, Estates Committee, *passim*, 1913, 315).

Museum

Apart from purchase of furniture to fit up a committee room and museum showcases (three for £17 10s. 6d in the first instance) little more needed to be spent initially to open the museum at Tudor House, which had evidently been thoroughly restored by Spranger.

Meanwhile, in May 1912 the Estates Committee had accepted the offer of Mr. R. E. Nicholas to act as honorary curator of the museum, appointing him "during the pleasure of the Council" (SBCM 1912, 713). Directories list Rowland Edgar Nicholas at Cobden House, Cobden Avenue, Bitterne Park between 1912 and 1920. He had by then presumably retired from his post with Toogoods, the seed merchants. A Fellow of the Linnean and Geological Societies, he was evidently a man of wide scientific and other interests, whose unpaid services must have been literally invaluable in the early stages of the museum.

The Hartley College Council agreed to transfer "articles of local interest" from the College museum to Tudor House. These "numerous and valuable articles" were scheduled and received by 24 June, when it was also reported that "the Hon. Curator was very busy visiting various institutions and collecting curios" (SBCM 1912, 791). Individual donations also increased the material gathered at Tudor House, including some of the items previously loaned for the 1904 "Relics" exhibition which prompted the developments leading eventually to the establishment of Southampton's first civic museum.

The Estates Committee invited the Mayor to open it officially on the afternoon of Monday, 29 July 1912. A "distinguished company" of nearly 100 persons attended the ceremony and celebratory tea. Introducing the Mayor, Edward Bance outlined the history of Tudor House (as written by Prof. Hearnshaw) and recalled how it had been acquired from Mr. Spranger, who had bought it, restored it and generously sold it to the Corporation. He stressed that the museum was "strictly a Hampshire one" and appealed for gifts or loans of suitable exhibits. He praised the work of Mr. Nicholas as voluntary curator and drew attention to the former cabbage garden behind the house having been made into an old English garden. The museum would be open to the public from 10 to 6 during the summer and 10 to 4 in winter — free on Tuesdays, Thursdays and Saturdays: on the other days there would be an admission charge of 6d.

Since 9 November 1911 the Mayor was Councillor Henry Bowyer. He seems to have changed his view since he led opposition to the Council acquiring Tudor House in March-April 1911, for he was reported (H Adv 3 August 1912) as saying "it behoved them in Southampton to do all they could to preserve ancient memories and relics of glorious history and maintain them for the benefit of children and future generations. He rejoiced that the borough council had secured Tudor House for them and was sure that posterity would congratulate them on that action."

The people of Southampton evidently appreciated the town's first museum. In September 1913 the Borough Council received the report of its Estates Committee which included an account by R. E. Nicholas of the first year of Tudor House (ST 13 September 1913); this stated that 18,400 people had signed the visitors' book there and that "probably quite twice that number had visited the house" (visitors in the 1980s number 60,000/70,000 a year). It was also reported that £30.10s. had been taken on "pay days" i.e. 1,220 sixpences — equivalent to well over £1 in present money terms. This represented an average of less than ten paying visitors on each of the three days a week that an admission charge was made. Alderman Bance told the council that in the first few months since its publication 1,958 copies of the history of Tudor House, a booklet by F. J. C. Hearnshaw, had been sold, along with 2,870 of the picture postcards of the house published by the Corporation.

Bance paid generous tribute to the work of Mr. Nicholas as honorary curator; not only was he most enthusiastic and efficient but he also spent his own money going to places on behalf of the museum, without wishing to be reimbursed. Nicholas served as honorary curator for over twenty years; Tudor House Museum must be greatly indebted to him for his pioneering contribution in this capacity, before the council appointed professional museum staff to build on the foundation he laid.

Conservation

After the thorough-going restoration of Tudor House around 1900 and the minor additions effected by the Corporation in connection with its opening as a museum in 1912, little further work on its maintenance was needed until the 1930s. Fifty years later, it became evident that to maintain and strengthen this much-visited historic building, a major programme of conservation and refurbishment was necessary, involving replacement of decayed and infested timbers and partial reconstruction of the fabric.

The first phase of this complex project was recently undertaken by G. E. Prince and Son Ltd., the four-generation family firm of Southampton builders which celebrated its centenary in 1986 and whose many contracts have included an increasing number of schemes for sensitively refurbishing old buildings.

Director Brian Prince served on the committee of the City of Southampton Society for ten years from 1974 and was its chairman in 1979-81; he was a prime mover in getting "listed" status accorded to South Western House. He took a close personal interest in the rehabilitation work at Tudor House and was warm in his praise of the quality of craftsmanship devoted to this time-consuming but satisfying project — "a fascinating job."

Work on a building of this age and form presented some unusual problems, not least handling large beams longer than its width! Cutting tenons and joints in oak beams over 300mm. square was no job for faint-hearted carpenters — but a taxing challenge to craftsmen skilled with their tools and prepared to sharpen and re-set them several times a day. In the reconstruction at Tudor House, only limited use was made of mechanical tools; traditional methods were generally adopted. Although some modern materials and techniques were employed to obtain better and stronger fixings and for insulation purposes, plastering, for example, reverted to the old-time use of animal hair in the render coats.

Restoration work at Tudor House, 1983-84.

APPENDIX

Admission Charges

From its opening on 29 July 1912 Tudor House Museum was free on Tuesdays, Thursdays and Saturdays, with an admission charge of 6d on other days.

Sir Sidney Kimber (1949, 22) later recalled that in 1914 "because of the out-of-the-way situation and cost of admission (the museum) was little known or used." He wrote, "I thought that if the charges, small as they were, were waived and the hours of admission extended, there might be more popularity, so I asked the Council to open it each week-day from 10 a.m. to 6 p.m., with free admission. After the matter had been referred to the Estates Committee, the proposal was at once put into operation. The attendance increased appreciably . . . "

Kimber's memory seems to have led him into error. Council minutes (SBCM 1914, 674, 764) and contemporary press reports show that at the Council meeting on 10 June 1914 Councillor Kimber's proposal was referred to the Estates Committee; on 7 July, with Kimber attending, this committee adopted his suggestion but when its recommendation came before the Council on 22 July an amendment was carried — on a show of hands — "that until the financial liabilities involved in the purchase of Tudor House are liquidated, the charges be continued as at present."

In support of the amendment it was said that free admission would lose the Council £100 a year (4,000 sixpences) and that £500 a year was paid out of the rates on Tudor House.

At a later date Wednesday was added to the "free days" but 6d was still charged on Mondays and Fridays until 1933. On 24 March the Public Libraries Committee considered a report on receipts from admission charges for the five years ending 31 December 1932. It evidently found that the income did not justify collection because it resolved "that in future Tudor House Museum be open free to the public upon all such days as the museum may be open." (Alderman Kimber was then among those present). This decision was duly confirmed by the Council, so that Tudor House became "open free daily as and from Saturday 1 April 1933" (SBCM 1933, 800, 957).

REFERENCES

Abbreviations

H Adv	Hampshire Advertiser
H Ind	Hampshire Independent
ST	Southampton Times
S Ref	Southern Reformer
SRO	Southampton City Record Office (Conveyances and leases, Tudor House)
SBCM	Southampton Borough Council Minutes (in SRO)
FSMG	Friends of Southampton Museums and Galleries Newsletter
DNB	Dictionary of National Biography
Proc HFC	Proceedings of Hampshire Field Club and Archaeological Society

Personal Information from

The Misses E. and M. Bance
G. M. W. Cotton
J. H. Foley
J. Cooper-Poole

Other Sources

Boase, F. 1965 *Modern English Biography,* London
Cotton, D. C. 1971 *St. Michael's Church,* Southampton
Crockford, 1882 etc *Clerical Directory,* London
Davies, J. S. 1883 *History of Southampton*
Englefield, H. 1801 *A Walk Through Southampton*
Godwin, G. N. (ed) 1900 *Mate's Illustrated Guide to Southampton*
Hearnshaw, F. J. C. (ed) 1904 *Relics of Old Southampton*
Kimber, S. G. 1949 *Thirty-eight Years of Public Life in Southampton*
Mitchell, E. A. ('Townsman') 1938 *Occasional Notes,* Southampton
Peberdy, P. S. 1957/67 *Tudor House Museum*
Pevsner, N. and Lloyd, D. 1967 *Hampshire and the Isle of Wight,* The Buildings of England series
Pike, W. T. (ed) 1905 *Hampshire at the Opening of the Twentieth Century,* Brighton
Platt, C. 1973 *Medieval Southampton,* London
Rance, A. 1980 *Southampton and its Museums*
Samuels, A. 1982 Sir Richard Lyster, *FSMG Newsletter,* 10
Southampton City 1986 *Official Handbook*
Southampton City n.d. (recent) *Visitors Guide*
Southampton Museums 1914-54 *Tudor House Museum*
Southampton Museums 1959 etc *Historic Buildings of Southampton*
Southampton Tourist Guides Assoc. n.d. (recent) *A Guided Talk around the Old Walled Town*
Spooner, H. 1968 *A History of Taunton's School*
Temple Patterson, A. 1962 *The University of Southampton*
Vale, J. 1983 *The Country Houses of Southampton,* Proc HFC 39, 171-190 (offprint)
Various eds 1848-1922 *Directories,* Hampshire and Southampton
1899-1902 *Southampton Annual.*

THE CITY OF SOUTHAMPTON SOCIETY

The City of Southampton Society was founded in 1962 and is recognised by the National Civic Trust. It is an independent body of people who care about their city and try to ensure:

(a) that new developments are carefully conceived and through high standards of design and town planning truly improve the urban environment;

(b) that wherever possible buildings of historic interest and the rich legacy of open spaces are preserved;

(c) that the informed opinion of Southampton people is expressed and brought to bear upon the local authorities in all matters affecting the city.

As a non-political voluntary association it derives its influence solely from the expertise and support of its members, whose annual subscriptions provide its main source of income.

Why not join us and strengthen our influence by your support?

For further details of the Society and its activities write to the Hon. Secretary, Mr. J. H. Guilmant, 24 Whitworth Road, Southampton SO2 4GF or telephone 227797.